TABLE OF CONTENTS

Page

ACRONYMS

CBP	United States Customs and Border Protection
DHS	United States Department of Homeland Security
DOD	United States Department of Defense
ISR	Intelligence, Surveillance, and Reconnaissance
JIATF	Joint Inter-agency Task Force
JP	Joint Publication
TCO	Transnational Criminal Organization
UAS	Unmanned Aerial System
USBP	United States Border Patrol

ILLUSTRATIONS

CHAPTER 1

INTRODUCTION

Background

Counter-narcotics has been a significant policy effort of the United States of

America since President Richard Nixon declared war on drugs in 1971. In March of

2009, Senator Joe Lieberman referred to Mexican Transnational Criminal Organizations

"a clear and present danger"[1] to the United States. As demand for illicit narcotics within

the United States remains high, Mexican Transnational Criminal Organizations (TCOs)

will continue to battle for control of border crossing points in the Southwest United

States, increasing the potential for violence to spill over into civilian communities along

that axis in the Southwest United States. The border between the United States and

Mexico runs approximately 2,200 miles from the Pacific Ocean in the west to the Gulf of

Mexico in the east. It divides the American states of California, Arizona, New Mexico,

and Texas from the Mexican states of Baja California Norte, Sonora, Chihuahua,

Coahuila, Nuevo Leon, and Tamaulipas. Much of the border is defined by the course of

the Rio Grande for 1,248 miles. The U.S.-Mexico border is the most frequently crossed

border in the world, with more than 350,000,000 legal crossings per year at 45 crossing

sites.

Violence against U.S. federal and state law enforcement personnel in the

Southwest Border Region has been steadily rising over the last decade. From 2004 to

2005, violent incidents against Customs and Border Patrol (CBP) agents increased 108

percent.[2] In 2006, CBP agents were the targets of 746 violent incidents including 435

incidents of rock assaults (known as "rockings"), 173 physical assaults, 46 vehicle

1

assaults, and 43 firearm assaults.[3] This is a radical departure from previous years when it was common for members or associates of the Mexican drug cartels to abandon their cargo when confronted by U.S. law enforcement personnel.

During the period from January 2007 to December 2010, Mexico has estimated that 34,500 Mexican citizens were killed in drug-related violence.[4] This spike in murders manifested itself in the wake of President Felipe Calderon's declaration of war on the Mexican drug cartels.[5] More than ten percent of those killed lived in Ciudad Juarez, a city of 1.3 million people located across the Rio Grande from El Paso, Texas. With more than 3,100 murders in 2010,[6] Ciudad Juarez was a more dangerous place to live than Afghanistan with a person being thirty times more likely to be murdered in Ciudad Juarez in 2010 than in Afghanistan per capita.[7] This is a startling illustration of the scope of violence growing closer and closer to the United States each year and prompting Sheriff Larry A. Dever of Cochise County, Arizona, to say: "Get the military on the border, and get them there now."[8]

To counter the proliferation of drug-related violence in the Southwest Border Region, the United States has implemented a plan known as the Merida Initiative to improve cooperation between U.S. and Mexican law enforcement counterparts.[9] As part of this program, U.S. Immigration and Customs Enforcement (ICE) agents work with their Mexican counterparts to help prevent the trafficking of drugs and persons from Central and South America into the United States. On 15 February 2011, two ICE agents were returning to the U.S. Embassy in Mexico City from a meeting with other U.S. law enforcement officials working with Mexican authorities when they were attacked by suspected Mexican drug cartel gunmen near the northern city of San Luis Potosi. Agent

Jaime Zapata was killed and his partner, Agent Victor Avila, was shot twice in the leg during the attack.[10] On February 24, six members of the Zetas cartel were arrested in connection with the shooting. U.S. reports indicate that the gunmen made comments before opening fire suggesting that they knew the two men were U.S. law enforcement agents. The suspect's confession, however, states that it was a case of mistaken identity. The Zetas had intended to ambush a rival cartel member who drove an SUV similar to the one that Agents Zapata and Avila were driving.[11] Regardless of which account is true, one thing is clear: U.S. citizens, even law enforcement agents, are not safe from the violence currently spreading through northern Mexico as drug cartels battle for possession of trafficking routes across the U.S.-Mexico border.

In order to help combat the threat of violence spilling across the border, the Department of Homeland Security (DHS) purchased three Predator B drones in October of 2011 to augment the fleet of seven it already owns and operates.[12] The funds for the purchase were approved after an August 2010 push by members of the Congressional Unmanned Systems Caucus, a group of fifty congressional representatives often called the "Drone Caucus." Of the fifty members of the Drone Caucus, ten were representatives from Southern California, the hub of Unmanned Aerial Systems (UAS) construction in the United States.

This purchase, at a cost of $32 million, was made without a provision to include additional pilots, ground crew, and maintenance support for the new aircraft. While they hope to eventually employ 18 to 24 drone aircraft along the borders, Homeland Security personnel admit that they lack the personnel to fly the new Predator Bs and analyze the actionable intelligence they gather. Due to a lack of qualified crews, the Department of

Homeland Security is able to operate its current fleet of seven Predator B UASs only five days per week. Thus, it is unlikely that the new aircraft will have a significant impact on the ability of the United States to effectively secure its borders. Without an increase in the number of personnel assigned to operate and maintain the UASs and analyze the actionable intelligence they collect, the remote sensing capability of the DHS will not be sufficient to make a significant impact on the operations of Mexican TCOs or the national security of the United States.

Problem Statement

Since 2006, more than 30,000 Mexican citizens have died in drug-related violence. With the threat of this violence escalating and spilling across the border into the United States, it is necessary to employ the full range of assets and options available for the U.S. government to defeat or neutralize a growing national security threat to the safety and sovereignty of the United States.

National Security Threat

A national security threat comprises legal, military, and economic factors. For the purpose of this thesis, the national security threat to the United States posed by Mexican TCOs is defined as the combination of violent crime and the total economic impact on the United States. The violent crime used to assess the national security threat from Mexican TCOs includes assaults, murders, and robberies directly linked to activities by Mexican TCOs inside United States borders. The economic impact is the total monetary cost of law enforcement operations that specifically target the illegal drug trade, the cost of healthcare for drug addicts and the victims of violent drug-related crime, and lost revenues due to drug abuse.

<u>Significance</u>

It is estimated that nearly 90 percent of the cocaine that is destined for U.S. markets travels through the Mexico/Central America corridor,[13] due to its location between the world's largest producer of cocaine (Colombia) and the world's largest consumer of cocaine (the United States). In addition to cocaine, Mexico is the primary foreign supplier of marijuana and methamphetamines in the United States and is a major transit route for heroin.[14] These major sources of income have allowed Mexican drug cartels to challenge the legitimacy of Mexican government institutions near the U.S. border through the use of violence and intimidation.

On 13 August 2010, President Barack Obama signed the Southwest Border Security Bill in response to the immediate threats associated with the substantial increase in violence in Mexico resulting from conflict amongst Mexican TCOs and between Mexican TCOs and the Mexican government. In a speech announcing his signature of the bill, President Obama stated:

> I have made securing our Southwest border a top priority since I came to office. That is why my administration has dedicated unprecedented resources and personnel to combating the transnational criminal organizations that traffic in drugs, weapons, and money, and smuggle people across the border with Mexico.[15]

Mexican TCOs currently dominate the illicit drug trade within the United States, operating in more than 1,000 cities across all fifty states[16] (see map below). These operations include the purchase, sale, distribution, storage and security of "most of the heroin, marijuana, and methamphetamine available in the United States."[17] The National

Drug Intelligence Center (NDIC), part of the United States Department of Justice, assesses that major Mexican-based TCOs and their associates will continue to solidify their dominance of the U.S. wholesale drug trade as illustrated in figure 1. Mexican TCOs will maintain that dominance for the foreseeable future due to the competitive advantage of access to and control of smuggling routes across the U.S. Southwest Border.[18] This potential advantage over rival TCOs leads to violent confrontation and conflict within the Mexican TCOs as they struggle to expand their influence within the United States.

It is unclear how much influence is exerted by the drug cartels on Mexican government institutions near the U.S. border. Former U.S. Representative Tom Tancredo (R-CO) alleged in 2002 that he had "no doubt Mexican military units along the border are being controlled by drug cartels, and not by Mexico City. The military units operate freely, with little or no direction, and several of them have made numerous incursions into the United States."[19] According to a 2008 Department of Homeland Security Report, the Mexican military made 278 known border crossings into United States territory from 1996 to 2008.[20] Among these incidents was a 23 January 2006, incident in which individuals dressed in Mexican military uniforms, carrying military-style weapons, and using military vehicles interfered with and prevented U.S. law enforcement personnel from intercepting a drug shipment in Hudspeth County, Texas.[21]

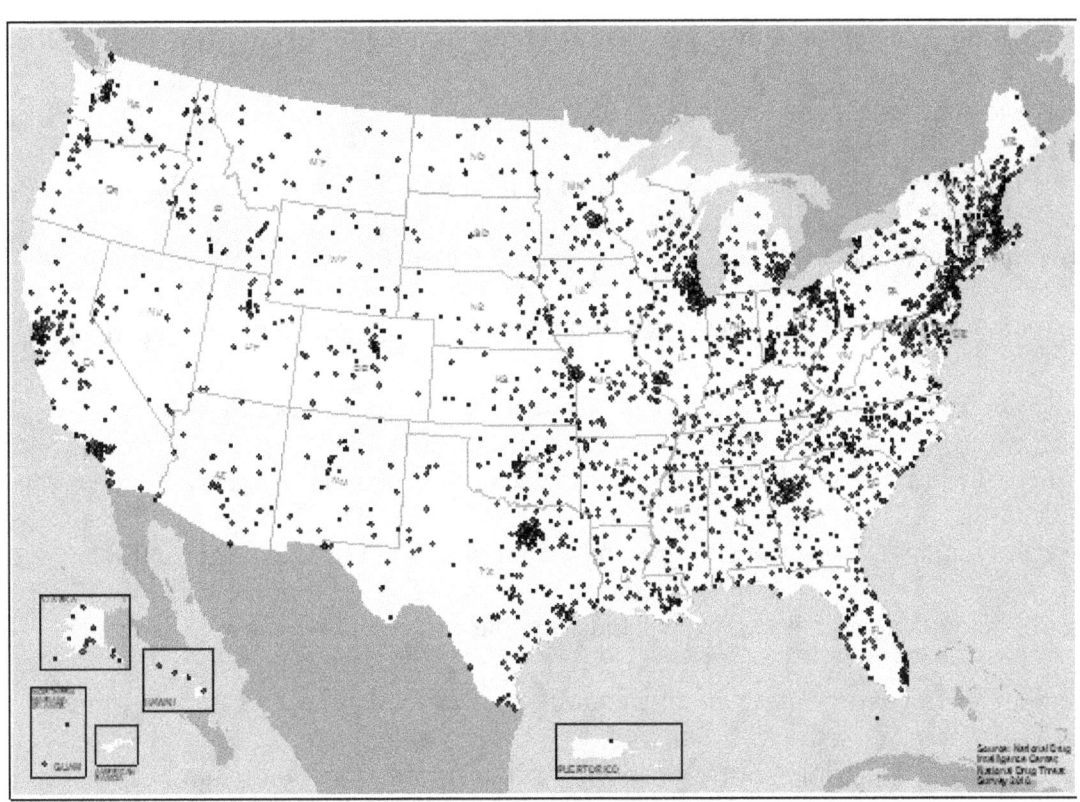

Figure 1.   Locations of Known Mexican TCO Operations in the United States

Source: National Drug Intelligence Center, *National Drug Threat Assessment 2011*
(Washington, DC: United States Department of Justice, 2011).

As of 2007, the economic impact of illicit drug use in the United States was more

than $193 billion.[22] In comparison, the United States spent $170.9 billion on the wars in

Iraq and Afghanistan in 2007,[23] making the War on Drugs the costliest war conducted by

the United States in terms of money. The same year, 1,019 U.S. service members died in

Iraq and Afghanistan while 38,371 Americans died of drug-induced causes (both legal

and illegal drugs).[24] In 2007, deaths from illicit drug use surpassed deaths due to

gunshots in the United States. Additionally, illicit drug use was the leading cause of death

in seventeen states and the District of Columbia, surpassing even motor vehicle accidents

in terms of lethality.[25] The war on drugs exceeds the cost of the war on terror in terms of

7

both financial resources and lives lost. It is clear that a concerted and unified effort at the federal and state level is required and necessary.

The federal government has consistently focused its efforts on reducing the supply of illegal narcotics to U.S. markets. From 2002 to 2009, the federal drug control budget grew from $10.8 billion to $25.6 billion, an increase of more than 200 percent.[26] Of that funding, 59 percent was allocated to supply reduction programs like drug interdiction while the remainder was spent on demand reduction programs like education and rehabilitation. Despite these efforts and the growth of the federal drug control budget, drug use among Americans age twelve and older has increased by nearly 16 percent.[27] With both federal expenditures on drug control and the number of U.S. citizens using drugs increasing at alarming rates, it is clear that the current drug control strategy is not working and change may be required.

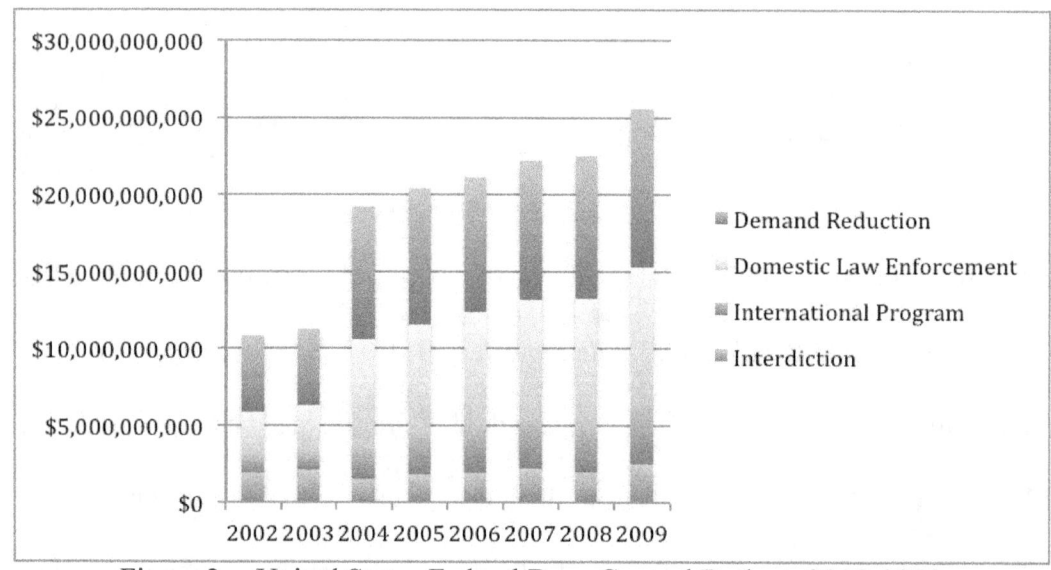

Figure 2.   United States Federal Drug Control Budget, 2002-2009
Source: Created by author

8

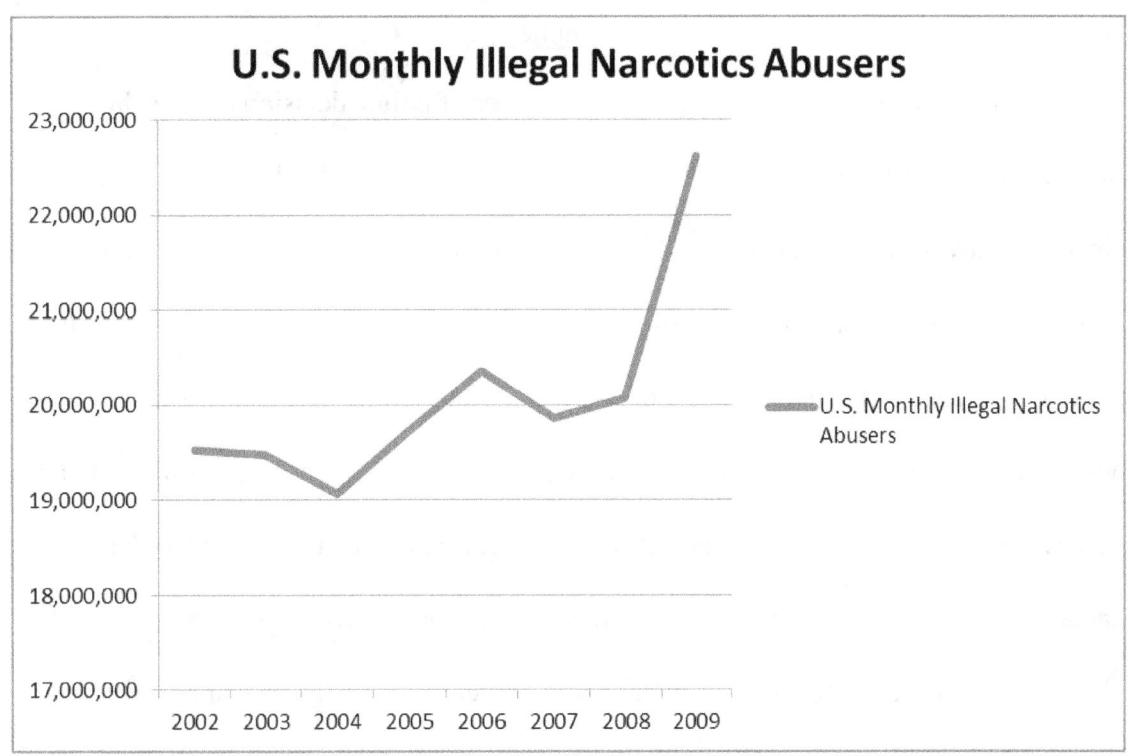

Figure 3.   Number of U.S. Citizens, ages twelve and up, who report using illicit narcotics in the last 30 days from 2002 to 2009

Source: Created by author

Research Questions

The primary research question used to solve the problem statement is: "In order to prevent the spread of violence by Mexican drug cartels, what should be the U.S. military role in securing the border in the Southwest United States?" A secondary research question that will be answered in the course of this thesis is: "What type of U.S. military units/assets should be used to help the Department of Homeland Security (DHS) secure the U.S.-Mexico border?"

9

Assumptions

Political pressure drives a significant number of policy decisions in the United States. What is important to voters is important to their political leaders, particularly as elections draw near. As such, one underlying assumption is that political pressure to secure U.S. borders, especially the border with Mexico, will continue to increase as drug-related violence continues to propagate. Another assumption is that, as the wars in Iraq and Afghanistan conclude, certain ISR assets like Aerostat balloons used to support base defense operations on military Forward Operating Bases will be redeployed to the U.S. and available for use to support Department of Homeland Security agencies securing the U.S.-Mexico border. A third assumption is that border security efforts can be unified across governmental agencies and departments to form one, cohesive doctrine to coordinate disparate law enforcement, intelligence, and military assets utilized to defend the U.S.-Mexico border. Finally, it is assumed that the government of Mexico will continue to serve as an ally in the effort to curtail drug-related violence and to secure the U.S.-Mexico border and not succumb to internal strife and collapse due to the power and influence of the drug cartels. Should the government of Mexico be unable to continue its efforts to curtail the spread of drug-related violence, the issue of border security becomes one of international relations (where the possibility of military intervention exists) rather than one of law enforcement.

Definitions

The following terms are defined below as used in the context of this thesis.

Aerostat Systems. Aerostat systems, like the ones manufactured by TCOM, L.P., of Columbia, Maryland, are unmanned tethered balloons that are used to provide

10

surveillance, early warning, and communications. They vary in size and payload capacity (from 200 lbs on the smallest model to 3,500 lbs on the largest model) and operate at altitudes of 1,000 to 15,000 feet depending on the size of the system. Each balloon is connected to a trailer on the ground by a Kevlar tether that uses fiber optic cables to transmit data over a secure network and provide power to the balloon's surveillance systems.[28] Aerostats are currently used in Iraq and Afghanistan by U.S. military forces and in Texas, New Mexico, Arizona, Florida, and Puerto Rico by DHS.

Department of Defense. An executive department of the United States responsible for providing the military forces needed to deter war and to protect the security of the United States. The DOD includes the Departments of the Army, the Navy, and the Air Force. These departments are responsible for the oversight, administration, and control of the United States Army (USA), the United States Navy (USN), the United States Air Force (USAF), and the United States Marine Corps (USMC).

Department of Homeland Security. An executive department of the United States with the primary missions of preventing terrorist attacks within the United States, reducing the vulnerability of the United States to terrorism, minimizing the damage caused by terrorist attacks perpetrated against the territory of the United States, and assisting in the recovery from terrorist attacks that do occur within the United States. DHS is also responsible for the protection of the borders of the United States. Key components of DHS include the United States Coast Guard (USCG), United States Customs and Border Protection (CBP), United States Immigration and Customs Enforcement (ICE), and the Transportation and Security Administration (TSA).

Intelligence, Surveillance, and Reconnaissance. An activity that synchronizes and integrates the planning and reconnaissance and operations of sensors, assets, and processing, exploitation, and dissemination systems in direct support of current and future operations. This is an integrated intelligence and operations function.[29]

Military Support to Civilian Law Enforcement Agencies (MSCLEA). A mission of civil support that includes support to civilian law enforcement agencies. This includes but is not limited to: combating terrorism, counterdrug operations, national security special events, and national critical infrastructure and key asset protection.

The *Posse Comitatus Act* (PCA). A federal law under Title 18 of U.S. Code that prohibits active duty military service members from being used to enforce the laws of the United States unless expressly authorized by the United States Constitution or the United States Congress. Under PCA, active duty service members may serve only in an advisory capacity to civilian law enforcement agents. National Guard units serving within the limits of Title 32 of U.S. Code or while under the direct authority of the state governor are not subject to the restrictions of PCA.

Predator Drone. An Unmanned Aerial System (UAS) developed and built by General Atomics Aeronautical Systems, Incorporated, in San Diego, California. The Predator is an unmanned aircraft with a payload capacity of more than 3,000 pounds. It can achieve speeds up to 275 miles per hour and cruise at 50,000 feet. Its primary purpose is as a reconnaissance platform, equipped with multiple cameras and sensors capable of identifying and tracking both vehicles and individuals. It can be equipped with precision-guided munitions, but the seven platforms operated by the Department of Homeland Security are used primarily for gathering intelligence and conducting surveillance and reconnaissance. Each system costs between $10 million and $11 million.[30]

Rocking. The act of throwing a rock or another hard object at a law enforcement agent with the intent of causing physical harm and interfering with the agent's execution of his duties with regard to drug and human trafficking interdiction.

Southwest Border Region. The area surrounding the U.S.-Mexico border, which stretches approximately 2,200 miles from the mouth of the Rio Grande at the Gulf of Mexico to the Pacific Ocean. It includes the U.S. states of Texas, New Mexico, Arizona, and California and the Mexican states of Baja California Norte, Sonora, Chihuahua, Coahuila, Nuevo Leon, and Tamaulipas.

Spillover Violence. Spillover violence entails deliberate, planned attacks by the drug cartels on U.S. assets, including civilian, military, or law enforcement officials, innocent U.S. citizens, or physical institutions such as government buildings, consulates, or businesses. This definition does not include trafficker-on-trafficker violence, whether perpetrated in Mexico or the U.S.

U.S. Northern Command (USNORTHCOM). A geographic combatant command within the Department of Defense (DOD) responsible for providing command and control of DOD homeland defense efforts and coordinating defense support of civil authorities. USNORTHCOM's mission is to conduct homeland defense, civil support, and security cooperation to defend and secure the United States and its interests. USNORTHCOM's Area of Responsibility includes the United States (except for Hawaii), Canada, Mexico, the Bahamas, Puerto Rico, the U.S. Virgin Islands, and portions of the Caribbean region.

Limitations

Information regarding the specific use of Intelligence, Surveillance, and Reconnaissance assets of the United States Department of Defense in support of U.S. border security is classified and unavailable for use in this thesis. The Department of Homeland Security, perhaps because it was only established in 2002, does not currently have a comprehensive border control doctrine for the employment of its personnel and equipment, much less the integration of assets from other agencies like the Department of Defense, the Department of Justice, National Guard, and state and local law enforcement. The Department of Homeland Security's Counternarcotics Doctrine is only eleven pages long, illustrating the fact that inter-agency cooperation in the realm of border security is not yet mature.

Delimitations

Historical research for this thesis was restricted to the time period from 2002, when the Department of Homeland Security was established by the *Homeland Security Act of 2002*, to the present. This focused the thesis on the period of time during which the current National Security apparatus has been in place. Additionally, research concentrated on how the Department of Defense and some of its key assets could best be integrated into U.S.-Mexico border security operations to enhance the effectiveness and efficiency of those operations. No attempt was made by the researcher to determine possible multi-national approaches or inter-agency solutions to the problem of border security that did not include the Department of Defense.

---

[1]CNN.com, "Senators: Obama Border Initiative Good Step, But Insufficient," 25 March 2009, http://articles.cnn.com/2009-03-25/politics/senate.mexico_1_

border-violence-drug-cartels-gun-show-loophole?_s-PM:POLITICS (accessed 18 November 2011).

[2]Michael T. McCaul, *A Line in the Sand: Confronting the Threat at the Southwest Border* (Washington, DC: House Committee on Homeland Security, Subcommittee on Investigations, 2006), 18.

[3]Ibid.

[4]Fox News Latino, "Death Toll in Drug-Plagued Mexican Border City Tops 3,100," 15 December 2010, http://latino.foxnews.com/news/2010/12/15/death-toll-drug-plagued-mexican-border-city-tops/ (accessed 4 September 2011).

[5]Clare R. Seelke and Kristin M. Finklea, *U.S.-Mexican Security Cooperation: The Merida Initiative and Beyond* (Washington, DC: Congressional Research Service, 2011), 9.

[6]Fox News Latino, "Death Toll in Drug-Plagued Mexican Border City Tops 3,100."

[7]Kelly Holt, "Facts Reveal Juarez is Deadlier Than Afghanistan," *The New American*, 1 March 2011, http://www.thenewamerican.com/index.php/world-mainmenu-36/6505-facts-reveal-juarez-is-deadlier-than-afghanistan (accessed 25 September 2011).

[8]James Heiser, "Juarez, Mexico, Murder Rate Up 40 Percent," *The New American*, 3 March 2011, http://www.thenewamerican.com/world-mainmenu-26/north-america-mainmenu-36/6543-juarez-mexico-murder-rate-up-40-percent (accessed 4 September 2011).

[9]Office of National Drug Control Policy, *National Southwest Border Counternarcotics Strategy* (Washington, DC: Executive Office of the President of the United States June 2009), 5.

[10]Dane Schiller, "ICE Agent Wounded in Mexico Attack Released from Houston Hospital," *Houston Chronicle*, 15 February 2011, http://www.chron.com/news/article/ICE-agent-wounded-in-mexico-released-from-1682313.php (accessed 4 September 2011).

[11]Fox News Latino, "Killing of ICE Agent Jamie Zapata Was Case of Mistaken Identity, Says Suspect," 24 February 2011, http://latino.foxnews.com/latino/news/2011/02/24/ice-agent-jamie-zapatas-alleged-killer-confesses-mexican-army-error (accessed 7 December 2011).

[12]Brian Bennett, "Homeland Security Adding 3 Drones Despite Lack of Pilots," *Los Angeles Times*, 26 October 2011, http://www.latimes.com/news/nationworld/nation/la-na-us-drone-20111027,0,1704002.story (accessed 14 November 2011).

[13]Office of National Drug Control Policy, *National Southwest Border Counternarcotics Strategy* (Washington, DC: Executive Office of the President of the United States June 2009), 17.

[14]Office of National Drug Control Policy, *National Drug Control Strategy* (Washington, DC: Executive Office of the President of the United States, 2011).

[15]Office of National Drug Control Policy, *National Drug Control Strategy*, (Washington, DC: Executive Office of the President of the United States, 2011).

[16]National Drug Intelligence Center, *National Drug Threat Assessment 2011* (Washington, DC: United States Department of Justice, 2011), 48.

[17]Ibid., 8.

[18]Ibid.

[19]Dave Gibson, "The U.S. Military Should Be Used to Defend Our Border with Mexico," Examiner.com, 28 January 2010, http://www.examiner.com/immigration-reform-in-national/the-u-s-military-should-be-used-to-defend-our-border-with-mexico (accessed 4 September 2011).

[20]Ibid.

[21]McCaul, 21.

[22]United States Department of Justice, *The Economic Impact of Illict Drug Use on American Society 2011* (Washington, DC: United States Department of Justice, 2011), ix.

[23]Amy Belasco, *The Cost of Iraq, Afghanistan, and Other War on Terror Operations Since 9/11* (Washington, DC: Congressional Research Service, 29 March 2011), CRS-3.

[24]Jiaquan Xu et al., *National Vital Statistics Reports* 58, no. 19 (Washington, DC: National Center for Health Statistics, 20 May 2010), 11.

[25]Centers for Disease Control and Prevention, *Special Tabulations From CDC's Wonder Database on Vital Statistics* (Atlanta: U.S. Department of Health and Human Services, Centers for Disease Control and Prevention, 2011).

[26]State University of New York–Albany, *Sourcebook of Criminal Justice Statistics*, 2011, http://www.albany.edu/sourcebook/pdf/t1142012.pdf (accessed 14 November 2011).

[27]drugwarfacts.org, "Drug Use Estimates," 2011, http://www.drugwarfacts.org/cms/?q=node/27 (accessed 14 November 2011).

[28]TCOM, "TCOM, Aerostats," 2011, http://www.tcomlp.com/aerostats.html (accessed 7 December 2011).

[29]Joint Chiefs of Staff, Joint Publication 2-01, *Joint and National Intelligence Support to Military Operations* (Washington, DC: Joint Chiefs of Staff, 5 January 2012), GL-12.

[30]General Atomics Aeronautical Systems, Inc., "Predator B UAS," 2011, http://www.ga-asi.com/products/aircraft/predator_b.php, (accessed 19 November 2011).

CHAPTER 2

LITERATURE REVIEW

Chapter 2, "Literature Review" is organized by topic. The three primary areas that relate to the thesis are border security, drug-related violence, and the use of ISR assets in support of border security operations.

Border Security

In order to gain a sense of the complexity of the issue of border security, one must become familiar with the national strategic documents that govern Homeland Security and Border Protection. These documents include *The National Security Strategy*, *The Southwest Border Counternarcotics Strategy*, and *National Drug Control Strategy*. Each of these documents establishes the unifying national security objectives set forth by the President of the United States. It is also necessary to understand the perspective of the United States Congress, who is responsible for funding the agencies who implement the president's national security objectives. To that end, it is important to conduct a review of Congressional subcommittee reports, publications by the Congressional Research Service, and federal law.

Law enforcement, inter-agency, and military operations are, by their nature, complex endeavors that require significant thought, planning, and resourcing. For this reason, U.S. law enforcement, intelligence, and military agencies establish doctrine for their operations in support of securing the homeland. This doctrine is intended to ensure unity of effort, establish continuity and consistency, and provide a common operating picture for all personnel participating in joint, inter-agency, and multi-national operations. A review of this doctrine is necessary to understand how the United States government secures its borders, protects its people, and utilizes the resources it has at its disposal. Before attempting to determine whether or not a system can work better, one must first understand how it is intended to work and what its ultimate objectives are, which is defined in national strategic documents.

Border security and immigration law are contentious issues in the current climate of American politics. This has resulted in a plethora of scholarly, legal, and editorial publications over the last decade, as well as the publication of numerous Congressional Research Service reports. A review of this literature helps inform the researcher of the climate in which policy is enacted and provides a guide for recommendations of change, if any. As an issue of interest to law enforcement and military professionals alike, numerous theses have been written by students at the Army War College, the Naval Postgraduate School, the Naval War College, the United States Command and General Staff College, and the School of Advanced Military Studies. A review of these documents helps inform the researcher of contemporary military and law enforcement thoughts on the subject. Additionally, organizations like the RAND Corporation, the Defense Science Board, and the Joint Advanced Warfighting School have published articles relating to the escalation of violence in the U.S. Southwest Border Region, the turmoil within Mexico, and the employment of military technology in support of law enforcement agencies and host nation security forces.

Colgen, LP, a defense consulting firm founded by MG (Ret) Robert Scales, PhD, and COL (Ret) Jack Pryor, published a strategic assessment of border security in Texas in September of 2011. The report, titled *Texas Border Security: A Strategic Military*

Assessment, was co-authored by GEN (Ret) Barry McCaffrey and MG (Ret) Scales and commissioned by Todd Staples, the Commissioner of the Texas Department of Agriculture. The report is a "military perspective on how to best incorporate strategic, operational and tactical measures to secure the increasingly hostile border regions along the Rio Grande River."[1]

Most of the literature to be reviewed concerning border security has been published within the last ten years. A significant reason for this is the increased concern that America's leadership has developed since the terrorist attacks on September 11, 2001. Publications regarding border security in the Southwest Border Region have become more common place since President Calderon of Mexico began his campaign to defeat the drug cartels within his country in 2006, which is when the drug-related violence in the northern states of Mexico began to escalate.

Newspapers from the Southwest Border Region, like the *Los Angeles Times*, the *Tucson Sentinel*, and the *Houston Chronicle* have all carried stories covering border security. Most of the articles recognize the complexity of border security and acknowledge that citizens living near the border are experiencing increasing concern due to the escalation of violence in Mexico. These publications have given voice to the local and national level political leaders who represent Texas, New Mexico, Arizona, and California, the majority of whom are calling for the federal government to send more resources to the border to improve security. As Mayor Raul Salinas of Laredo, Texas, said "I would welcome any resources and equipment that would help us to be more vigilant along the border. And if it's equipment that would provide support, I would welcome it with open arms."[2]

20

Drug-Related Violence

Drug-related violence is an issue of acute concern to both Mexican and American citizens living near the border between the two countries. As competition between drug cartels has intensified over the last five years, murder rates within Mexico have reached record levels. Additionally, violence directed towards American law enforcement and border patrol agents has risen during the same time period.

Concerns are particularly high among local law enforcement officials who live and work in the Southwest Border Region. Media outlets from the local to national level have covered the acts of violence as the fight between Mexican cartels over control of border crossing sites continues to expand. Law enforcement officials in Texas, New Mexico, and Arizona have been particularly vocal in their quests to prevent the violence from spreading into their jurisdictions. The sheriffs of Hudspeth County, Texas, Luna County, New Mexico, and Cochise County, Arizona, have all expressed concern over the possibility of spillover violence being introduced into their communities. While Sheriff Devers of Cochise County, Arizona, called for military forces to be deployed to the border as soon as possible, Sheriff Raymond Cobos of Luna County, New Mexico, is concerned that New Mexico is not doing enough to ensure the security of its border. Texas, Arizona, and California are "banging their drums while we're using a popsicle stick. . . . The possibility [there's] going to be a catastrophic civil war in Mexico is pretty high, and I have to face the probability that at some point I have to deal with it."[3]

Studies conducted by the Department of Justice, the Centers for Disease Control and Prevention, and independent websites like DrugWarFacts.org illustrate the rising cost of drug-related violence in terms of both lives lost and financial cost. A comprehensive, scholarly source regarding drug-related violence is the State University of New York (SUNY)–Albany Sourcebook of Criminal Justice Statistics. The Sourcebook of Criminal Justice Statistics tracks information regarding everything from budget allocations for federal agencies to historical trends in drug-related violence throughout the United States. The information provided by the Sourcebook is invaluable to any researcher attempting to ascertain trends in federal, state, and local expenditures and law enforcement statistics on a national level.

The Use of Military Assets in Border Security

Information regarding the specific use of military assets, especially ISR assets, in roles supporting border security operations is somewhat limited by the sensitive nature of the subject. Much has been written editorially, however, about the acquisition of such systems for use by the Department of Homeland Security to prevent violence from spreading into the United States due to conflicts between Mexican drug cartels.

Political leaders from the Southwest Border Region have been clear on their opinions regarding the use of military equipment redeployed to the United States from Iraq and Afghanistan for use along the border with Mexico. Most, like U.S. Representatives Henry Cuellar (D-TX), Candice Miller (R-MI), Michael McCaul (R-TX), and Sheila Jackson Lee (D-TX), are supportive of U.S. military ISR assets being transferred to border security roles upon their return from combat zones in the Middle East. Representative Jackson Lee went so far as to state that she is interested in using military personnel with experience in operating and maintaining such ISR assets in support of civil authorities. "I'm not so inclined to ignore this talent . . . and let it dissipate when we are confronting threats unknown," Jackson Lee said.[4]

Legislation was introduced by Representative Ted Poe (R-TX) on 15 November 2011, known as the Send Equipment for National Defense Act. The legislation requires the Department of Defense to transfer at least ten percent of the UASs, night vision goggles, and high mobility multi-purpose wheeled vehicles (HMMWVs) returning to the United States from Iraq to federal and state law enforcement agencies within one year of its redeployment. The purpose of this equipment transfer is to strengthen border security along the U.S.-Mexico Border.[5] Mayor John Cook of El Paso, Texas, expressed his concern that the legislation amounts to a militarization of the border between the United States and Mexico that could hinder relations between the two countries and damage the countries' economic partnership.[6]

General capabilities for the various ISR systems are readily available through their manufacturers' web sites. Information about the cost, payload capacity, operational range, and speed of the Predator B UAS is published on the General Atomics Aeronautical Systems, Inc., products page. Vital statistics about Aerostat systems are available through the web sites of their various producers, like TCOM LP, Lockheed Martin, and ILC Dover and through the U.S. Army and U.S. Air Force official web sites. Defense contractors like Qual-Tron, Inc., provide information regarding various types of unattended ground sensors, which can be used to monitor vehicle traffic and movement by people on foot through remote areas that are difficult to patrol consistently.

While border security has always been a concern, the increasing violence in northern Mexico over the last five years has caused a surge in media coverage, political debate, scholarly review, and academic research into the state of affairs in the Southwest Border Region. Lawmakers, particularly those from Texas, New Mexico, Arizona, and

California, have expressed their opinion that the federal government needs to increase its efforts to secure the border with Mexico using all resources available, including military personnel and equipment. Local law enforcement officials have also indicated their desire for military assistance to enhance border security by citing the increasing levels of violence employed by members of Mexican drug cartels and the availability of resources returning from war zones in Iraq and Afghanistan.

---

[1]Barry McCaffrey and Robert Scales, *Texas Border Security: A Strategic Military Assessment* (Austin, TX: Colgen, LP, 2011), 1.

[2]Julian Aguilar, "Mayors Disagree About War-Zone Equipment on Border," *Tuscon Sentinel*, 21 November 2011, http://www.tusconsentinel.com/local/report/112111 _tx_mayors_border/mayors-disagree-war-zone-equipment-border/ (accessed 7 December 2011).

[3]Teri Schultz, "More Drone Patrolling U.S.-Mexico Border," *Tuscon Sentinel*, 7 December 2011, http://www.tusconsentinel.com/local/report/120711_border_drones/ more-drones-patrolling-us-mexico-border/ (accessed 9 December 2011).

[4]Elizabeth Titus, "Lawmakers Want Defense Techonology on Border," *Tuscon Sentinel*, 18 November 2011, http://www.tusconsentinel.com/nationworld/report/111811 _border_defense_technology/lawmakers-want-defense-technology-border (accessed 8 December 2011).

[5]Ted Poe, *House Resolution 3422: The Send Equipment for National Defense Act*, (Washington, DC: United States House of Representatives, 15 November 2011), 1.

[6]Julian Aguilar, "Mayors Disagree About War-Zone Equipment on Border," *Tuscon Sentinel*, 21 November 2011, http://www.tusconsentinel.com/local/report/112111 _tx_mayors_border/mayors-disagree-war-zone-equipment-border/ (accessed 7 December 2011).

CHAPTER 3

RESEARCH METHODOLOGY

Introduction

The qualitative research methodology used in this thesis is the case study. In a qualitative case study, the researcher conducts "an intensive, holistic description and analysis of a single instance, phenomenon, or social unit."[1] This method allowed for a comprehensive and thorough review of the facts concerning border security in the U.S. Southwest Border Region with respect to Mexican drug cartels. Volumes of data on the economic and security impacts of the drug trade on American society already exist as compiled by various federal agencies and institutions. There was no need to duplicate the work already completed by organizations with resources that far outstrip those of the individual researcher. Though this method did restrict the amount of information available for use in the thesis, the amount of information already in existence was more than sufficient to evaluate the national security impact of the Mexican drug cartels and formulate a thesis on how best to counter them.

Using the case study methodology, the researcher focused on the specific area of the Southwest Border Region and the challenges facing the American and Mexican governments in that region. The case, in the context of this research, was current U.S. border control strategy, specifically in the Southwest Border Region. Data was collected through a review of literature on the topics of border security, drug-related violence, and the use of specialized intelligence, surveillance, and reconnaissance assets in a role supporting border security. The literature reviewed consisted of documents, archival records, review of interview transcripts, and observations.

25

Data Collection

In the context of this research, the documents consisted of national strategic documents produced by the federal government of the United States and doctrinal publications from homeland security, law enforcement and military agencies of the United States. The archival records reviewed were the published statistics regarding the spread of drug-related violence attributed to Mexican TCOs published by scholarly legal sources like the SUNY-Albany Sourcebook for Criminal Justice Statistics, data on the spread of drug abuse and drug-related mortality developed by the Centers for Disease Control and Prevention, and institutional records from the Department of Homeland Security detailing their successes and failures in ensuring border security.

Interview records with prominent security analysts were examined by studying media coverage and editorial essays published on the topics of border security, drug-related violence, and the controversy regarding the use of military equipment and personnel supporting civil law enforcement in the Southwest Border Region. Finally, observations by local law enforcement agents, political leaders, and social commentators were reviewed to help determine which methods and resources are most effective in protecting the U.S.-Mexico border.

The first step in this methodology is to collect the data pertinent to the case study. This required an examination of the agencies and departments responsible for securing the borders of the United States and their contributions to national security with respect to the Southwest Border Region. These departments and agencies include the Executive Office of the President of the United States, the United States Congress, the Department of Homeland Security and its components, the Department of Justice and its components, the Department of Defense and its components, the United States National Guard, and state and local law enforcement.

Data Analysis

The second step in this methodology is to analyze whether current capabilities and measures undertaken by the United States government are sufficient to combat the threat posed by the Mexican drug cartels. It was also necessary to analyze the effectiveness of the joint and inter-agency doctrine that governs the collective efforts of these organizations. Next, the researcher examined the growing number of National Guard soldiers and support operations in a border security role to assess the effectiveness of inter-agency operations in the Southwest Border Region.

The third step in this methodology is to determine whether or not assets currently exist within the structure of the United States government to enhance the effectiveness and efficiency of border security efforts in the Southwest United States. These assets need not necessarily be limited to equipment and technology. They may also include personnel available to be used in support of border security.

This research methodology should allow for a comprehensive and unbiased review of the Southwest Border Region security efforts enacted by the United States government with regard to the national security threat posed by Mexican drug cartels. The thesis statement requires a complete and thorough review of published historical data, joint and inter-agency doctrine, and national strategy in order to fully-analyze the threat posed by Mexican drug cartels to national security. This analysis should allow for a determination of whether or not current efforts are sufficient to counter the growing threat of the Mexican drug cartels and what, if anything, can and should be done to improve the national security of the United States.

Standards of Quality and Verification

In an attempt to eliminate bias and maintain objectivity in the context of the study, the researcher collected data from both public and private sources, including some sources from both sides of the U.S.-Mexico border in order to ensure that one perspective does not sway the research or its conclusions. To that end, peer review and triangulation were the primary methods used to ensure standards of quality and verification in this case study.

Peer Review. Throughout the case study, the researcher must ensure the validity and reliability of both his research and his recommendations. Internal reliability is established through triangulation, member checks, peer examination, and the reduction of bias. Peer review provided an external check of the researcher's process and the reliability of his/her conclusions.[2] The intent of peer review was for the peer reviewer to serve as a sort of devil's advocate, keeping the researcher honest and ensuring that the researcher's conclusions made sense and were consistent with the analysis of the data collected.[3] In this case study, peer reviews were conducted by asking fellow students and instructors at the Command and General Staff School to read the researcher's thesis and provide their feedback on the analysis and recommendations provided.

Triangulation. Triangulation uses multiple sources of data to confirm emerging findings. "In triangulation, researchers make use of multiple and different sources, methods, investigators, and theories to provide corroborating evidence. Typically, this process involves corroborating evidence from different sources to shed light on a theme or perspective."[4] In this case study, triangulation involved the collection and analysis of American and Mexican strategic documents relating to border security, opinions expressed in writing and spoken word by local leaders, and a review of relevant statistics compiled by reputable researchers.

Finally, the researcher attempted to reduce bias in order to ensure the validity and reliability of the case study. To this end, the researcher reviewed a broad variety of literature to gather the data necessary to analyze the current situation in the Southwest Border Region as it relates to the national security threat posed by Mexican TCOs. Statistics were reviewed from both the United States government and from academic institutions like the State University of New York at Albany. Prevailing political and law enforcement opinions were gathered from a variety of media sources and federal legislation in both the United States and Mexico.

---

[1]Sharan B. Merriam, *Qualitative Research and Case Study Applications in Education* (San Francisco: Jossey-Bass Publishers, 1998), 27.

[2]John W. Creswell, *Qualitative Inquiry and Research Design: Choosing Among Five* Traditions (Thousand Oaks, CA: SAGE Publications, Inc., 1998), 202.

[3]Ibid.

[4]Ibid.

CHAPTER 4

ANALYSIS

Introduction

Once literature has been reviewed and the research methodology has been designed, it is necessary to analyze the data collected. In the context of this case study, data is analyzed in order to solve for the underlying issues related to the problem statement: "With the threat of violence escalating and spilling across the border into the United States, it is necessary to employ the full range of assets and options available for the U.S. government to defeat or neutralize a growing national security threat to the safety and sovereignty of the United States."

Data is analyzed with a focus toward answering the primary and secondary research questions: "In order to prevent the spread of violence by Mexican drug cartels, what should be the U.S. military role in securing the border in the Southwest United States?" and "What type of U.S. military units/assets should be used to help the Department of Homeland Security (DHS) secure the U.S.-Mexico border?"

The research methodology requires the researcher to determine the scope of the national security threat posed by the Mexican drug cartels. This threat may include the economic impact of drug abuse by American citizens, physical attacks by cartel members against U.S. citizens and law enforcement agents, and the potential for the destabilization of the Mexican government. It is necessary to establish that the Mexican drug cartels constitute a significant threat to United States national security that cannot be defeated or deterred by law enforcement methods alone in order to justify an expanded role for the Department of Defense in securing U.S. borders. This must be proven before any determination of what role Department of Defense personnel and equipment should play in border security can be considered. This need can be measured by analyzing statistics related to border security, the national sovereignty of Mexico, drug-related crime on both sides of the U.S.-Mexico border, drug abuse within the United States, and the economic and cultural interdependence of the United States and Mexico.

Discussion

One way to determine the future security threat posed by the Mexican drug cartels is to assess the impact of federal budgets on border security operations. Proving that sufficient resources must be allocated to the Department of Homeland Security to deter or defeat the national security threat posed by Mexican drug cartels will make a strong case for maintaining those funds in an era of shrinking federal budgets.

Another way to determine the significance of the national security threat posed by the Mexican TCOs is to demonstrate whether or not narco-trafficking organizations within Mexico constitute an insurgency against the Mexican government. If it can be shown that the government of Mexico is in danger of collapsing due to insurgent activity (either through violent intimidation of government officials or outright rebellion) within its own borders, an argument could be made to increase the presence of U.S. military units along the Southwest Border. This deployment of troops would be done in order to prevent spillover violence and to help ensure the security of our southern neighbors through security assistance programs to the government of Mexico.

The United States and Mexico are close in more than just proximity. Politically, culturally, and economically, the two countries are inextricably linked. Persons of Hispanic descent are the fastest growing demographic in the United States. Of that

31

population, persons of Mexican descent in particular are the largest segment. From 2000 to 2010, the Mexican-American population increased by 54 percent, growing from 20.6 million people to 31.8 million people.[1] Mexican Americans, according to the 2010 U.S. Census, now account for approximately 10 percent of the total population of the United States. In fact, the growth in the Mexican American demographic accounted for 41 percent of the population growth in the United States from 2000 to 2010.[2]

More than $460 billion in trade passed between the two countries in 2011, making Mexico the United States' third largest trading partner, accounting for 12.5 percent of all foreign trade.[3] Through February of 2012, the United States and Mexico are on pace to conduct more than $470 billion in trade.[4] Since the implementation of NAFTA on 1 January 1994, trade between the United States and Mexico has increased by more than $360 billion per year, averaging nearly 10 percent growth annually.

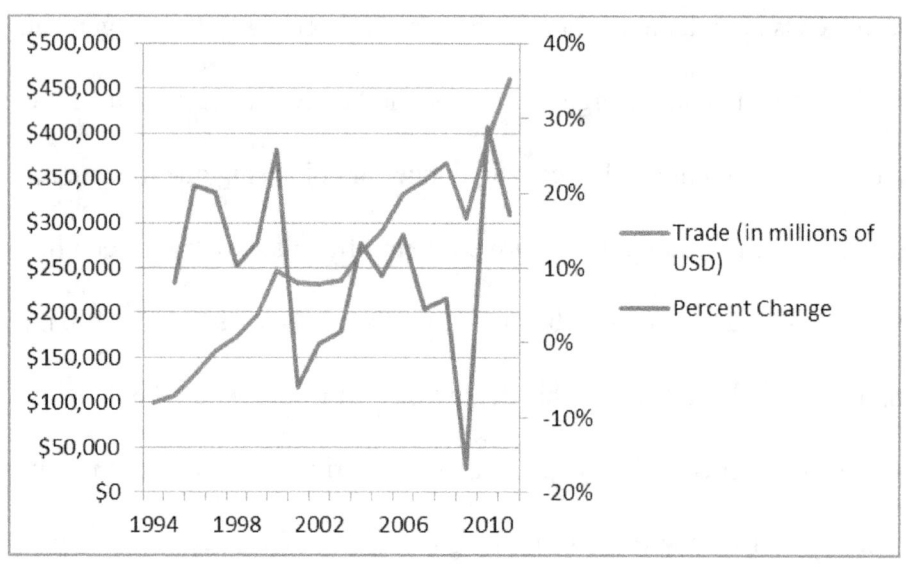

Figure 4.   Trade (in Millions of USD) Between the United States and Mexico from 1994-2011

Source: Created by author

32

Recent trends in immigration and population increases indicate that Mexican Americans account for the lion's share of population growth in the United States. The increasing interdependence of Mexico and the United States through NAFTA has formed a strong cultural and economic bond between the two countries. Nearly 350,000,000 people legally transit the U.S.-Mexico border each year, making it the busiest border in the world. The preservation of a bi-national relationship founded on economic interdependence, shared culture, and mutual support must be maintained. The maintenance of this relationship requires improved security in the Southwest Border Region to remove the greatest point of contention between the United States and Mexico.

U.S. narcotics consumption results in profits of $39 billion per year flowing back across the border into Mexico,[5] strengthening the drug cartels. The economic cost of America's drug addiction is estimated at $215 billion annually,[6] exceeding the highest annual economic cost of the wars in Iraq and Afghanistan combined by more than 20 percent.[7] Clearly, America has a drug problem. The Mexican drug cartels are capitalizing on U.S. drug consumption to make enormous sums of money. As of 2009, 59 percent of counternarcotics expenditures were directed toward supply reduction programs, while only 41 percent focused on demand reduction programs.[8] Despite increasing levels of spending on supply reduction programs, drug use amongst Americans over the age of twelve continued to increase, growing nearly 16 percent from 2002 to 2009.[9]

Given the close proximity to their primary consumer, the Mexican drug cartels have established a competitive advantage over other drug smuggling criminal organizations by securing control of illegal border crossing sites into the United States from Mexico. By using some of their profits to legally obtain firearms in the United

33

States to subvert Mexico's more stringent gun control laws, the Mexican drug cartels have driven their competition out of the Southwest Border Region through the use of force. Los Zetas, in particular, are well-known for their use of violence to eliminate competition and intimidate local authorities. Originally formed by members of the Mexican Army's Special Forces, Los Zetas' operations now encompass most of Mexico's Gulf Coast and extend into Guatemala and the southwestern United States[10]. Los Zetas' rise to power in eastern Mexico brought them into conflict with the Gulf Cartel and the Sinaloa Cartel, resulting in a large portion of the drug-related violence in Mexico.

Since 1999, the U.S. Border Patrol has steadily increased in size in terms of both personnel and budget. The U.S. Border Patrol increased its budget by a factor of three[11] and its force of Border Patrol Agents by a factor of nearly five from 1999 to 2011.[12] Over the period of these budget and personnel increases, the number of illegal alien apprehensions of Mexican citizens attempting to enter the United States fell by more than 80 percent.[13] This decrease, while partially attributable to the growing economic strength of Mexico relative to the United States, is also due in part to the increasingly successful efforts of the U.S. Border Patrol to secure the Southwest Border.

While a slowing American economy and the efforts of the U.S. Border Patrol have served to reduce illegal immigration over the past twelve years, they have done little to curb the growth of Mexican drug cartels' influence in the United States. Due in large part to the amount of money to be made in U.S. markets, Mexican drug cartels have established operations in more than 1,000 cities across all fifty states.[14] Illegal narcotics have become a big business for the Mexican cartels because of their control of smuggling routes with access to the lucrative American market. In fact, the cartels operate much like

34

businesses, training key personnel in Mexico and then deploying them across the border into the United States in order to establish market territories across the country in conjunction with American street gangs, who facilitate distribution of their products.[15]

In order to maintain this immensely profitable business, the Mexican drug cartels seek to remain under the radar of American law enforcement agencies, keeping a tight lid on drug-related murders on the American side of the border. This is not true however, of other drug-related crimes like kidnapping and extortion. Phoenix, Arizona, has been particularly hard hit, experiencing more than 370 kidnapping cases in 2008 alone.[16] The majority of the victims are illegal aliens or persons involved in the drug trade, which serves to keep the focus of federal law enforcement agencies on terrorist threats rather than cartel-on-cartel violence in the United States. The Mexican cartels-or their American gang affiliates–concentrate their violent activities against rivals, kidnapping them and ransoming them back to their families in an effort to intimidate each other and secure vital smuggling routes to major U.S. population centers. The grisly results of the failure to pay the ransoms in time have been discovered frequently in Phoenix, as dismembered bodies are investigated by Phoenix Police Chief Andy Anderson and his officers.[17]

The Mexican government reported in January of 2012 that 47,515 Mexican citizens have been killed in fighting between rival drug cartels since December of 2006[18] as the cartels struggle for dominance of the smuggling routes into the United States. A significant problem related to this surge in violent crime within Mexico is the ready availability of firearms in the United States. Mexican drug cartels frequently purchase firearms legally in the United States due to stricter gun control laws in Mexico. According to the U.S. Bureau of Alcohol, Tobacco, Firearms, and Explosives, more than

35

70 percent of the nearly 30,000 firearms seized by the Mexican government in 2009 and 2010 were purchased in the United States.[19]

While violent crime rates in Mexico continue to remain alarmingly high, there is no evidence to conclude that the Mexican government is in imminent danger of collapsing. The drug cartels, thus far, seem content to undermine local government and law enforcement in order to maintain their influence over smuggling routes into the United States, but do not appear to be a threat to the federal government. The people of Mexico, disenchanted with the current ruling party, still have faith in their federal institutions, as evidenced by the intense three-candidate presidential election scheduled for 1 July 2012.[20]

Analysis of Data–Primary Research Question

The researcher must first analyze data in relation to the primary research question: "In order to prevent the spread of violence by Mexican drug cartels, what should be the U.S. military role in securing the border in the Southwest United States?" In analyzing data related to the primary research question, the researcher focused on the development of a comprehensive border security doctrine and the establishment of a joint inter-agency task force for border security as the roles in which the military could make the greatest positive impact in border security operations.

Border Security Doctrine- Current doctrine related to border security, particularly where the Department of Defense is involved, is an issue of contention between the Departments of Defense and Homeland Security. The Department of Defense provides military assistance when legal authorities allow and resources are available, whereas the Department of Homeland Security has a continuous mission to ensure border security.[21]

Department of Defense officials have expressed concerns about the absence of a comprehensive strategy for Southwest Border security and the resulting challenges to identify and plan a military role in supporting border security operations.[22] Homeland Security officials have observed that military border assistance has been ad hoc due to the Department of Defense's other operational requirements.[23] Based on opinions provided to the Government Accountability Office by Defense and Homeland Security officials, it appears that current border security doctrine does not provide enough clarity on how military units should be employed to support Homeland Security agencies.

Joint Inter-agency Task Force for Border Security- The Department of Defense currently operates three joint task forces charged with supporting civil authorities in a counternarcotics capacity: Joint Inter-agency Task Force-West (JIATF-West), Joint Inter-agency Task Force-South (JIATF-South), and Joint Task Force-North (JTF-North). JIATF-West focuses on the geographical area including the Pacific Rim and Asia and is subordinate to U.S. Pacific Command. JIATF-South focuses on the Caribbean, Central America, and South America and is subordinate to U.S. Southern Command. JTF-North is responsible for all support to federal law enforcement agencies combating transnational threats in the approaches to the United States homeland. In practice, JTF-North focuses on counternarcotics operations in support of federal law enforcement agencies in the Southwest Border Region. JTF-North has a limited operating budget of $10 million annually–an amount which has remained virtually fixed since the late 1980s[24]-with which to provide this support.[25] Given that the Department of Defense budget for counternarcotics operations is $1.1 billion per year, it would seem that the allotment for

JTF-North to provide counternarcotics support to federal law enforcement agencies nationwide is somewhat low.[26]

The Merida Initiative is a program where the United States has provided more than $1.3 billion in aid to the government of Mexico since the initiative's inception in 2007.[27] In addition to direct economic support, the United States has provided training and equipment to Mexico for the purpose of improving counter-narcotics operations. The equipment provided includes both rotary-wing and fixed-wing aircraft, ISR aircraft, railroad x-ray inspection machines, polygraph machines, and computer equipment.[28] According to a Government Accountability Office report to the leadership of the House and Senate Armed Services Committees, increasing Department of Defense participation in programs like the Merida Initiative has the potential to improve inter-agency coordination and cooperation within the federal agencies of the United States government, strengthening military-to-military relationships with Mexico, and deterring illegal activity along the border.[29]

Analysis of Data–Secondary Research Question

After analyzing data in relation to the primary research question, the researcher must focus on the secondary research question: "What type of U.S. military units/assets should be used to help the Department of Homeland Security (DHS) secure the U.S.-Mexico border?" In analyzing the data, the researcher focused on three specific types of military equipment that the Department of Defense could use to greatest effect in supporting border security operations: intelligence analysis systems, ground penetrating radar, and biometric data systems.

Intelligence Analysis-Despite increases in the number of personnel employed by the U.S. Border Patrol and the amount of funding they receive, the Department of Homeland Security as a whole lacks a robust intelligence analysis capability. The amount of information gathered by Customs and Border Protection's Predator-B drones and Aerostat balloons can overwhelm the ability of their analysts to make sense of what has been collected and distill it into a useful product for agents in the field to use in the execution of their duties. Active duty and National Guard units are deployed to the Southwest Border Region on a frequent basis to provide intelligence support to civil authorities because of their expertise and the computer software they possess to quickly analyze and prioritize information. The employment of military intelligence units in a Defense Support to Civil Authorities capacity will help DHS analyze all of the data collected by providing a force multiplier that can enhance border security.

Ground Penetrating Radar-A common tactic used by Mexican drug cartels to avoid detection and interdiction by U.S. Border Patrol agents is to build and use tunnels running under the border. Many of these tunnels are dug as side shafts off of the drainage systems on the U.S. side of the border, making their detection from the surface difficult at best. Beginning in 2009, the Department of Homeland Security began to pursue acquiring ground penetrating radar for the U.S. Border Patrol through a partnership with Lockheed-Martin.[30] The U.S. Border Patrol's expertise in the use of ground penetrating radar is by no means robust. The U.S. Army Corps of Engineers, however, does possess a robust capability to use ground penetrating radar. In recent years, ground penetrating radar has been used to locate weapons caches and hideouts in Iraq and Afghanistan. More recently, the Corps of Engineers used ground penetrating radar in South Korea as part of an Eighth

39

Army effort to determine whether or not Agent Orange was buried at Camp Carroll in the late 1970s when the chemicals ceased to be used by the U.S. military.[31] If ground penetrating radar has the capability to locate barrels buried more than thirty years ago in South Korea, it certainly has the capability to detect tunnels built under the U.S.-Mexico border.

Biometrics-The Customs and Border Protection service currently uses an identification system called the Enforcement Case Tracking System (ENFORCE), which uses the 10-Print fingerprint system to establish the identity of both legal and illegal aliens and visitors to the United States.[32] This system does not allow for an illegal immigrant apprehended at the border to be identified on-site by U.S. Border Patrol agents. Instead, the fingerprint information must be scanned and sent to the regional Border Patrol office for analysis. The Department of Defense uses two biometric identification systems to positively identify personnel: the Biometric Automated Toolset System (BATS) and the Handheld Inter-agency Identification Detection Equipment (HIIDE). BATS and HIIDE allow the user to scan a subject's iris, photograph the subject for facial recognition software, and record the subject's fingerprints. Each system is equipped with a ruggedized laptop computer that connects to a nationwide database and is capable of confirming a person's identity in a matter of minutes (as long as the person's biometric data is already recorded in the database). These biometric systems would provide a more rapid identification system for Border Patrol agents to use in tracking repeat offenders and violent criminal aliens at the point of apprehension. Due to the extensive use of the BATS and HIIDE systems by military personnel during the wars in Iraq and Afghanistan, the Department of Defense is able to provide a capability bridge to augment and train U.S. Border Patrol agents until their biometric capability is sufficient to run the system without assistance.

Summary

Border security in the Southwest United States is an increasingly inter-agency effort. The complex nature of inter-agency relationships and the relative youth of the Department of Homeland Security further complicate border security operations. In May 2010, President Obama announced his plan to deploy an additional 1,200 National Guard soldiers to the borders shared by Mexico with Texas, New Mexico, Arizona, and California.[33] He also asked Congress to approve a plan to expand the United States Customs and Border Protection force by 1,500 border patrol agents[34]. Senator John McCain (R-AZ) introduced legislation allocating an additional 3,000 National Guard soldiers to be deployed to Arizona and 3,000 others to be deployed to Texas, New Mexico, and California.[35]

The increasing deployments of active duty and National Guard soldiers to support border security operations underscore the need for a comprehensive border security strategy. This strategy should be developed at the Department of Homeland Security level with oversight from the Obama administration and include the design and structure of a Joint Inter-agency Task Force for Border Security. Following the implementation of this government-wide border security strategy, the new JIATF-Border Security needs to develop its own doctrine to clearly define how assets from other federal agencies will be integrated into border security operations. This doctrine must address how military assets can be used to their best immediate effect through the use of capabilities like intelligence analysis, ground penetrating radar, and biometric systems.

[1]Sharon R. Ennis, Merarys Rios-Vargas, and Nora G. Albert, *The Hispanic Population: 2010* (Washington, DC: United States Department of Commerce, United States Census Bureau, May 2011), 2.

[2]Ibid.

[3]United States Census Bureau, *Foreign Trade: U.S. Trade with Mexico*, 2012, http://www.census.gov/foreign-trade/balance/c2010.html, (accessed 17 April 2012).

[4]Ibid.

[5]Richard A. Serrano, "Mexican Drug Cartels Setting Up Shop Across U.S.," *Los Angeles Times*, 17 April 2011, http://articles.latimes.com/2011/apr/17/nation/la-na-crack-house-20110417 (accessed 17 April 2012).

[6]Carol Cratty, ""Mexico Drug Cartels Extend Reach in U.S., CNN.com, 26 March 2010, http://articles.cnn.com/2010-03-26/us/drug.trends_1_drug-cartels-mexican-border-drug-violence?_s=PM:US (accessed 17 April 2012).

[7]Belasco, CRS-3.

[8]State University of New York–Albany, *Sourcebook of Criminal Justice Statistics*, 2011, http://www.albany.edu/sourcebook/pdf/t1142012.pdf (accessed 14 November 2011).

[9]drugwarfacts.org, *Drug Use Estimates*, 2011, http://www.drugwarfacts.org/cms/?q=node/27 (accessed 14 November 2011).

[10]InsightCrime.org, *Los Zetas*, InsightCrime.org, 2012, http://insightcrime.org/criminal-groups/mexico/zetas (accessed 17 April 2012).

[11]United States Border Patrol, *Enacted Border Patrol Program Budget by Fiscal Year*, 2011, http://www.cbp.gov/linkhandler/cgov/border_security/border_patrol/usbp_statistics/budget_stats.ctt/budget_stats.pdf (accessed 17 April 2012).

[12]United States Border Patrol, *Border Patrol Agent Staffing by Fiscal Year*, 2011, http://www.cbp.gov/linkhandler/cgov/border_security/border_patrol/usbp_statistics/staffing_92_10.ctt/staffing_92_11.pdf (accessed 17 April 2012).

[13]United States Border Patrol, *Total Illegal Alien Apprehensions by Fiscal Year*, 2011, http://www.cbp.gov/linkhandler/cgov/border_security/border_patrol/usbp_statistics/99_10_fy_stats.ctt/99_11_fy_stats.pdf (accessed 17 April 2012).

[14]National Drug Intelligence Center, *National Drug Threat Assessment 2011* (Washington, DC: United States Department of Justice, 2011), 48.

[15]Richard A. Serrano, "Mexican Drug Cartels Setting Up Shop Across U.S.," *Los Angeles Times*, 17 April 2011, http://articles.latimes.com/2011/apr/17/nation/la-na-crack-house-20110417 (accessed 17 April 2012).

[16]Brian Ross, Richard Esposito, and Asa Eslocker, "Kidnapping Capital of the U.S.A.," abcnews.com, 11 February 2009, http://abcnews.go.com/Blotter/story?id=6848672&page=1#.T7GXlO1yEll (accessed 17 April 2012).

[17]Ibid.

[18]Damien Cave, "Mexico Updates Death Toll in Drug War to 47,515, but Critics Dispute the Data," *The New York Times*, 11 January 2012, http://www.nytimes.com/2012/01/12/world/americas/mexico-updates-drug-war-death-toll-but-critics-dispute-data.html (accessed 17 April 2012).

[19]Evan Perez, "Mexican Guns Tied to U.S.: American-Sourced Weapons Account for 70% of Seized Firearms in Mexico," *The Wall Street Journal*, 10 June 2011, http://online.wsj.com/article/SB10001424052702304576375961350290734.html (accessed 17 April 2012).

[20]E. Eduardo Castillo, "Old Party Has Big Lead in Mexico Presidential Race," *The Miami Herald*, 2 May 2012, http://www.miamiherald.com/2012/05/02/2778793/old-party-has-big-lead-in-mexico (accessed 17 April 2012).

[21]Davi M. D'Agostino, *Observations on the Costs and Benefits of an Increased Department of Defense Role in Helping to Secure the Southwest Land Border* (Washington, DC: United States Government Accountability Office, 12 September 2011), 4.

[22]Ibid., 3.

[23]Ibid., 4.

[24]Ibid., 13.

[25]Ibid.

[26]Ibid.

[27]Jess Ford, *Merida Initiative: The United States Has Provided Counternarcotics and Anticrime Support but Needs Better Performance* Measures (Washington, DC: United States Government Accountability Office, July 2010), 4.

[28]Ibid., 8.

[29]D'Agostino, 3.

[30]National Science Foundation, "Border Patrol Agents to Spot Tunnels With Advance Ground-Penetrating Radar," *U.S. News and World Report*, 1 July 2009, http://www.usnews.com/science/articles/2009.07/01/border-patrol-agents-to-spot-tunnels-with-advanced-ground-penetrating-radar (accessed 17 April 2012).

[31]Ashley Rowland, "Army Using Ground-Penetrating Radar to Look for Agent Orange at Korea Base," *Stars and Stripes*, 2 June 2011, http://www.stripes.com/news/pacific/korea/army-using-ground-penetrating-radar-to-look-for-agent-orange-at-korea-base-1.145330 (accessed 17 April 2012).

[32]U.S. Customs and Border Protection, *Secure Borders, Safe Travel, Legal Trade: U.S. customs and Border Protection Fiscal Year 2009-2014 Strategic* Plan (Washington, DC: United States Customs and Border Protection, 2008), 18.

[33]*St. Petersburg Times*, Politifact.com Truth-o-meter, 29 July 2010, http://www.politifact.com/truth-o-meter/statements/2010/john-mccain/john-mccain-said-he-would-add-3000-troops-border-w/ (accessed 23 October 2011).

[34]Ibid.

[35]Ibid.

CHAPTER 5

CONCLUSIONS AND RECOMMENDATIONS

The final step in this methodology is to recommend a course of action to improve the border security of the Southwest Border Region of the United States based on the analysis of the data collected to answer the primary and secondary research questions. In this chapter, the researcher will review the problem statement, provide a discussion of pertinent conclusions, recommend courses of action related to the primary and secondary research questions, and summarize the findings contained in this thesis.

The researcher must maintain a focus on the problem statement in order to make logical conclusions and provide relevant recommendations. The problem statement in this case study is: "With the threat of violence escalating and spilling across the border into the United States, it is necessary to employ the full range of assets and options available for the U.S. government to defeat or neutralize a growing national security threat to the safety and sovereignty of the United States." Data was analyzed to answer the primary and secondary research questions: "In order to prevent the spread of violence by Mexican drug cartels, what should be the U.S. military role in securing the border in the Southwest United States?" and "What type of U.S. military units/assets should be used to help the Department of Homeland Security (DHS) secure the U.S.-Mexico border?"

Discussion

The gravity of the problem faced at the borders and the need to ensure America's national security could justify consolidating resources, personnel, and funding across departmental boundaries within the federal government. The recommended course of action may include the development, publication, and adoption of a new joint and inter-agency doctrine to coordinate efforts across the spectrum of law enforcement and national defense cooperation, the use of military equipment and personnel to augment the efforts of civilian law enforcement personnel in border security, or a combination of both. As the Binational Task Force on the United States-Mexico Border noted in the Executive Summary of its report on managing border security between the two countries:

> The United States is the principal destination for drugs coming from Mexico and the principal source of guns and bulk cash from criminal activities flowing into Mexico. Mexico is the principal, proximate source of illegal drugs coming into the United States, as well as the principal destination for guns illegally purchased in and shipped from the United States. Both countries suffer as a result of this symbiotic contraband trade, and both have an obligation to help contain it. Moreover, closer collaboration will bring greater success on this front than would additional unilateral effort, however vigorous.[1]

Any change in the nature of the U.S.-Mexico border must be weighed against the political and economic impacts such a decision would entail. The United States and Mexico, through the North American Free Trade Agreement (NAFTA) share a symbiotic relationship that is reflected in the border between the two countries being the busiest on Earth.

Mexico and the United States disagree on the nature of the growth of the Mexican drug cartels. Mexico believes that the cartels have grown powerful as a result of demand for illegal narcotics within the United States. The United States believes that the cartels have grown powerful as a result of the Mexican government's inability to police its side of the Southwest Border Region. Both countries agree that the cartels present a significant security threat that must be dealt with quickly and decisively.

Anticipated reductions in federal spending in the United States further complicate the issue of border security. Federal agencies are in competition for fewer resources as the president and Congress attempt to reduce the growth of the national deficit and guide the United States out of a recession. Any recommendations for further action to increase border security must take into account diminished resources, which necessitates inter-agency solutions. Resources must also be allocated according to the necessity of the spending. Organizations like Joint Task Force-North (JTF-North) should be funded based on an analysis of the missions they execute in support of civilian law enforcement agencies, not on a fixed budget pre-determined by funds available to the Department of Defense as a whole.

Recommendations

Primary Research Question

Improvements in border security must begin with the development and implementation of a comprehensive border security strategy developed by the Department of Homeland Security with oversight from the Obama administration. Input should be provided by all significant contributors, including the Departments of Defense, Justice, Agriculture, Commerce, Education, and Health and Human Services. This strategic document must clearly define the supported and supporting relationships in border security operations in order to prevent conflict between executive agencies.

Joint Inter-agency Task Force for Border Security-Included in this new border security strategy should be a directive to establish a Joint Inter-agency Task Force (JIATF) for Border Security that is funded as part of the Department of Homeland Security. This JIATF would be led by the Department of Homeland Security with support from other federal executive departments. The Department of Defense's contribution to JIATF-Border Security should include JTF-North as a supporting agency. Similar organizations already exist to combat narcotics smuggling from South America and Asia. According to a Government Accountability Office report to members of the Senate and House Armed Services Committees, such an organization could provide an opportunity for increased law enforcement cooperation, an improved military to military relationship between the United States and Mexico, and a significant deterrent to illegal activity at the border[2].

This new organization, JIATF-Border Security, should be funded through a new National Defense Authorization Act that authorizes military personnel to provide defense support to civil authorities for border security, rather than just counternarcotics. JIATF-Border Security's budget should be based on an analysis of projected mission requirements, rather than a fixed sum of less than $10 million per year[3]. JIATF-Border Security could be modeled on military support the U.S. Border Patrol in efforts like Operation Nimbus II. During Operation Nimbus II, elements of the 1st Battalion, 44th Air Defense Artillery Regiment, and 6th Squadron, 1st Cavalry Regiment, served under the operational control of JTF-North in coordination with the Arizona Joint Field Command, a component of U.S. Customs and Border Protection[4]. With a model structure already in place in Arizona, the Department of Homeland Security could quickly integrate military support to augment border security operations.

Border Security Doctrine-Once established, JIATF-Border Security must develop its own doctrine for integrating all available federal assets designated for border security operations. A comprehensive border security doctrine must be developed to efficiently integrate all federal agencies with a role in border security. The Department of Defense has published strategic documents at the joint and service levels to govern military support to civil authority (JP 3-28 at the joint level and FM 3-28 at the Army level). In order to ensure integration of all federal assets, the Departments of Homeland Security, Justice, Defense, Education, Commerce, Agriculture, and Health and Human Services should develop an inter-agency doctrine to clearly define each department's role in border security. Such a document would provide strategic purpose and direction for inter-agency operations in border security and prevent perceptions of ad hoc military support of civil law enforcement. Much of the groundwork has already been laid by Joint Publication 3-28 (Civil Support) and Army Field Manual 3-28 (Civil Support Operations). An inter-agency panel consisting of personnel from each federal department concerned with border security could develop inter-agency doctrine consistent with the Border Security Strategy.

Secondary Research Question

The security of the U.S.-Mexico border as it relates to illegal immigration has improved significantly since the establishment of the Department of Homeland Security in 2002. Increases in budget and personnel have allowed the U.S. Border Patrol to improve security throughout the Southwest Border Region. The creation of JIATF-Border Security and its implementation of a comprehensive border security doctrine will allow for immediate benefits in inter-agency cooperation, especially between the Departments of Homeland Security and Defense. These benefits are maximized in the areas of intelligence analysis, the use of ground penetrating radar to locate tunnels under the U.S.-Mexico border, and biometric data collection capability at the local level for Border Patrol agents.

Intelligence Analysis-The Department of Defense can support DHS border security efforts by providing an intelligence analysis capability that DHS does not currently possess. Active military intelligence units could be tasked to support JTF-North's counternarcotics operations in support of civilian law enforcement. These units can be temporarily provided to JTF-North for the purpose of analyzing intelligence collected by DHS assets focused on identifying illegal border crossing sites, allowing U.S. Border Patrol agents to focus their patrol and interdiction efforts on the most trafficked routes. Military intelligence units can also provide much-needed expertise in the maintenance and operation of UASs, bolstering the Department of Homeland Security's own capabilities.

Ground Penetrating Radar-Units throughout the Department of Defense possess ground penetrating radars that can identify trafficking tunnels running below the U.S.-Mexico border. On a periodic basis, DOD units can be deployed to the Southwest Border Region to support JTF-North with ground penetrating radars to confirm or deny the presence of new tunnels bypassing border security posts. These rotations can be funded by JTF-North (especially if their budget is based on operations rather than a fixed amount), allowing DOD units to preserve their own training budgets while having an opportunity to get their soldiers realistic experience that directly relates to their core mission.

Biometric Data Collection-U.S Border Patrol agents do not have a system capable of providing them on-site feedback for the identification of personnel they have apprehended attempting to illegally cross into the United States. Agents must currently relay information to their home patrol station for analysis and identification. DOD units possess two biometric systems that can help streamline this process: the Biometric Automated Toolset System (BATS) and the Handheld Inter-agency Identity Detection Equipment (HIIDE). Each system allows the user to create a database containing biometric information like fingerprints, iris/retina scans, and facial imaging to identify potential cartel members. This information is updated via a rugged laptop computer that compiles the biometric data, matches it with the suspect's name, and transmits the collected data to a national-level database that can be accessed by all other BATS and HIIDE systems. Used in Iraq and Afghanistan to screen potential local national employees against known insurgents, BATS and HIIDE systems could be transferred to DHS for use in border security under the auspices of the SEND Act.

Summary and Conclusions

The United States and Mexico are economically interdependent and–due to legal immigration and population growth–increasingly culturally linked. Each country's well-being is directly impacted by the other. As the United States and Mexico grow closer, the relationship between the two national governments becomes more important.

The supply-focused counternarcotics program used by the United States is not working. Despite increasing expenditures, drug abuse among Americans continues to grow. The number of admitted illegal narcotics abusers increased by 16 percent[5] despite more than 200 percent growth in federal spending on drug control from 2002 to 2009.[6] Part of the problem with focusing on supply rather than demand is that the strategy treats the symptoms rather than the disease. As long as demand for illegal narcotics in the United States remains high, Mexican drug cartels will have a lucrative market for their products and the Mexican government will have a difficult time curtailing drug-related violence within their borders.

Further research should be conducted to determine if the federal government should allocate a greater portion of its expenditures on counternarcotics programs toward demand reduction initiatives. As long as demand exists for illegal narcotics, cartels will continue to find a way to supply the habit. Increasing funding to youth-oriented programs like D.A.R.E. (Drug Abuse Resistance Education) in American schools can help deter drug abuse before it begins and improve access to quality rehabilitation programs for drug addicts to help prevent recidivism.

The number of firearms that cross the border from the United States to Mexico for use by the drug cartels is troubling. More than 21,000 firearms were legally purchased by agents of Mexican drug cartels from vendors in the United States in 2009 and 2010.[7] Research should be conducted to determine whether a change to United States gun control laws is feasible, acceptable, and necessary to reduce the flow of firearms to Mexico. This research may provide insights into reducing the level of violent crime in Mexico related to the illicit drug trade.

Additional study should also be conducted to determine the whether or not the United States should change the level of funding for its multi-national efforts to reduce the supply of illegal narcotics in North and South America. Programs like Plan Colombia and the Merida Initiative have improved host nation law enforcement and military capabilities in the counternarcotics arena. Stopping production at its source will yield greater results than attempting to interdict the supplies of narcotics as they cross the U.S.-Mexico border. To that end, Joint Inter-agency Task Forces-West (Pacific Rim and Asia) and –South (Central and South America) should increase their multi-national counternarcotics operations to destroy drug supplies at their sources with assistance from host nation partners.

Bi-national cooperation between the United States and Mexico is made somewhat difficult because of the differing roles played by law enforcement agencies and the military in each country. In Mexico, the Army is much more active in counternarcotics operations due to the infiltration and intimidation of local law enforcement by the drug cartels. Programs like the Merida Initiative, however, are bearing fruit by providing expert advice, professional training, and mission essential equipment to Mexican authorities for the purpose of combating the drug cartels. The targeting of ICE Agents Jaime Zapata and Victor Avila may indicate that the cartels see this increase in cooperation between the United States and Mexico as a direct threat to their operations.

Continuing to fund the Merida Initiative could improve cooperative intelligence collection, analysis, and sharing between the United States and Mexico. Combined with the establishment of JIATF-Border Security, the Merida Initiative could create significant results in the counternarcotics efforts of both the United States and Mexico. Such a task force could also improve direct coordination between the United States and Mexico, allowing for a greater impact on the cartels through the conduct of mutually-supporting and simultaneous counternarcotics operations.

At the outset of the case study, the researcher assumed that the best way to secure the United States border with Mexico would be to place troops on the border to deter illegal activity and prevent terrorist infiltration of the homeland. After months of research and study, it has become clear that border security is far too complex an issue to solve through the application of military force. Militarizing the border would have broad economic, cultural, political, and legal ramifications. There are key areas in which the military can provide critical support to civil law enforcement agencies in order to prevent the spread of drug-related violence without permanently damaging U.S.-Mexico relations and infringing on the civil liberties of American citizens. Developing a comprehensive, inter-agency doctrine will enhance the effectiveness and efficiency of agencies and personnel employed in border security operations. Establishing a joint inter-agency task force to coordinate all border security efforts will allow the federal government to use its funds and assets effectively in an era of shrinking budgets. Using military personnel and equipment to assist civil authorities in the key areas of intelligence analysis, the employment of ground penetrating radar, and the use of military biometric systems will provide training to civil law enforcement personnel and a necessary bridge until those capabilities exist within the Department of Homeland Security.

With presidential elections taking place in both Mexico (July) and the United States (November) in 2012, border security will likely be a key issue for candidates to confront. The threat posed by the Mexican TCOs to the national security of the United States demands that action be taken to improve border security. The people of the United States and Mexico simply cannot afford to allow the Mexican TCOs to continue to grow more powerful as thousands die in drug-related violence in the Southwest Border Region each year. Swift action must be taken in order to ensure national security and economic prosperity for each country.

---

[1]Robert C. Bonner and Andres Rozental, *Managing the United States-Mexico Border: Cooperative Solutions to Common Challenges* (Los Angeles: Pacific Council on

International Policy, Consejo Mexicano de Asuntos Internacionales, A.C., Binational
Task Force on the United States-Mexico Border, 2009), 12.

[2]D'Agostino, 3.

[3]Ibid., 13.

[4]Keith Anderson, "JTF-North Deploys Soldiers to Support Border Patrol in N.M.,
Ariz.," Army.mil, 27 March 2012, http://www.army.mil/article/76607/ (accessed 17 April
2012).

[5]drugwarfacts.org, "Drug Use Estimates," http://www.drugwarfacts.org/
cms/?q=node/27 (accessed 14 November 2011).

[6]State University of New York–Albany, *Sourcebook of Criminal Justice
Statistics*, 2011, http://www.albany.edu/sourcebook/pdf/t1142012.pdf (accessed 14
November 2011).

[7]Evan Perez, "Mexican Guns Tied to U.S.: American-Sourced Weapons Account
for 70% of Seized Firearms in Mexico," *The Wall Street Journal*, 10 June 2011,
http:// online.wsj.com/article/SB10001424052702304576375961350290734.html
(accessed 17 April 2012).

BIBLIOGRAPHY

Aguilar, J. "Mayors Disagree About War-Zone Equipment On Border." Tuscon Sentinel.com. 21 November 2011. www.tusconsentinel.com/local/report/112111_tx_mayors_border/mayors-disagree-war-zone-equipment-border/(accessed 7 December 2011).

Anderson, Keith. JTF-North deploys Soldiers to support Border Patrol in N.M., Ariz. San Antonio: U.S. Army. 27 March 2012. http://www.army.mil/article/76607/ (accessed 17 April 2012).

Belasco, Amy. *The Cost of the War in Iraq, Afghanistan, and Other War on Terrorism Operations Since 9/11.* Washington, DC: Congressional Research Service, 2011.

Bennett, Brian. "Homeland Security Adding 3 Drones Despite Lack of Pilots." *Los Angeles Times*, 26 October 2011. www.latimes.com/news/nationworld/nation/la-na-us-drone-20111027,0,1704002.story (accessed 14 November 2011).

Bonner, Robert C., and Rozental, Andres. *Managing the United States-Mexico Border: Cooperative Solutions to Common Challenges.* Los Angeles: Pacific Council on International Policy. 2009.

Castillo, E. Eduardo. "Old Party Has Big Lead in Mexico Presidential Race." *The Miami Herald*, 2 May 2012. http://www.miamiherald.com/2012/05/02/2778793/old-party-has-big-lead-in-mexico (accessed 17 April 2012).

Cave, Damien. "Mexico Updates Death Toll in Drug War to 47,515. but Critics Dispute the Data." *The New York Times*, 11 January 2012. http://www.nytimes.com/2012/01/12/world/americas/mexico-updates-drug-war-death-toll-but-critics-dispute-data.html (accessed 17 April 2012).

Center for Disease Control and Prevention. *Special tabulations from CDC's Wonder database on vital statistics.* Atlanta. GA: Department of Health and Human Services. 2011.

CNN.com. "Senators: Obama border initiative good step. but insufficient." 25 March 2009. http://articles.cnn.com/2009-03-25/politics/senate.mexico_1_border-violence-drug-cartels-gun-show-loophole?_s-PM:POLITICS (accessed 18 November 2011).

Cratty, Carol. "Mexico drug cartels extend reach in U.S." 26 March 2012. http://articles.cnn.com/2010-03-26/us/drug.trends_1_drug-cartels-mexican-border-drug-violence?_s=PM:US (accessed 17 April 2012).

Creswell, John W. *Qualitative Inquiry and Reserach Design: Choosing Among Five Traditions.* Thousand Oaks. CA: Sage Publications, Inc. 1998.

D'Agostino, Davi M. *Observations on the Costs and Benefits of an Increased Department of Defense Role in Helping to Secure the Southwest Land B*order. Washington. DC: United States Government Accountability Office, 2011.

drugwarfacts.org. "Drug Use Estimates." 2011. www.drugwarfacts.org/cms/?q=node/27 (accessed 14 November 2011).

Ennis, Sharon R., Merarys Rios-Vargas, and Nora G. Albert. *The Hispanic Population: 2010.* Washington. DC: United States Census Bureau. 2010.

Ford, Jess. *Merida Initiative: The United States Has Provided Counternarcotics and Anticrime Support but Needs Better Performance Measures.* Washington, DC: United States Government Accountability Office. 2010.

Fox News Latino. "Death Toll In Drug-Plagued Mexican Border City Tops 3,100." 15 December 2010. http://latino.foxnews.com/news/2010/12/15/death-toll-drug-plagued-mexican-border-city-tops/ (accessed 4 September 2011).

————. "Killing of ICE Agent Jamie Zapata Was Case of Mistaken Identity, Says Suspect". 24 February 2011. latino.foxnews.com/latino/news/2011/02/24/ice-agent-jamie-zapatas-alleged-killer-confesses-mexican-army-error (accessed 7 December 2011).

General Atomics Aeronautical Systems, Inc. "Predator B UAS." 2011. http://www.ga-asi.com/products/aircraft/predator_b.php (accessed 19 November 2011).

Gibson, Dave. "The U.S. military should be used to defend our border with Mexico." *The Examiner.* 28 January 2010. http://www.examiner.com/immigration-reform-in-national/the-u-s-military-should-be-used-to-defend-our-border-with-mexico (accessed 4 September 2011).

Heiser, James. "Juarez, Mexico Murder Rate Up 40 Percent." 3 March 2011. *The New American.* http://www.thenewamerican.com/world-mainmenu-26/north-america-mainmenu-36/6543-juarez-mexico-murder-rate-up-40-percent (accessed 4 September 2011).

Holt, Kelly. "Facts Reveal Juarez is Deadlier Than Afghanistan." *The New American.* 1 March 2011. http://www.thenewamerican.com/index.php/world-mainmenu-26/north-america-mainmenu-36/6505-facts-reveal-juarez-is-deadlier-than-afghanistan (accessed 25 September 2011).

InsightCrime.org. "Los Zetas." 2012. http://insightcrime.org/criminal-groups/mexico/zetas (accessed 17 April 2012).

McCaffrey, Barry, and Robert Scales. *Texas Border Security: A Strategic Military Assessment.* Colgen. LP. Austin, TX: Texas Department of Agriculture, 2011

McCaul, Michael T. *A Line in the Sand: Confronting the Threat at the Southwest Border.* House Committee on Homeland Security. Subcommittee on Investigations. Washington, DC: United States House of Representatives, 2006.

Merriam, Sharan. *Case Study Research in Education: A Qualitative Approach.* San Francisco: Jossey-Bass Publishers. 1998.

National Drug Intelligence Center. *National Drug Threat Assessment 2011.* Washington, DC: Department of Justice. 2011.

National Drug Intelligence Center. *The Economic Impact of Illicit Drug Use on American Society 2011.* Washington, DC: Department of Justice. 2011.

National Science Foundation. "Border Patrol Agents to Spot Tunnels With Advanced Ground-Penetrating Radar." *U.S. News and World Report.* 1 July 2009. http://www. usnews.com/science/articles/2009.07/01/border-patrol-agents-to-spot-tunnels-with-advanced-ground-penetrating-radar (accessed 17 April 2012).

Office of National Drug Control Policy. *National Drug Control Strategy.* Washington, DC: Executive Office of the President of the United States. 2011.

———. *National Southwest Border Counternarcotics Strategy 2011.* Washington, DC: Executive Office of the President of the United States. 2011.

Perez, Evan. "Mexican Guns Tied to U.S.: American-Sourced Weapons Account for 70% of Seized Firearms in Mexico." *Wall Street Journal.* 10 June 2011. http://online.wsj.com/article/SB10001424052702304576375961350290734.html (accessed 17 April 2012).

Poe, Ted. *House Resolution 3422: The Send Equipment for National Defense Act.* Washington, DC: United States House of Representatives. 15 November 2011.

Ross, Brian, Richard Esposito, and Asa Eslocker. "Kidnapping Capital of the U.S.A." 29 February 2009. http://abcnews.go.com/Blotter/story?id=6848672&page= 1#.T7GXlO1yEll (accessed 17 April 2012).

Rowland, Ashley. "Army Using Ground-Penetrating Radar to Look for Agent Orange at Korea Base." *Stars & Stripes.* 2 June 2011. http://www.stripes.com/ news/ pacific/korea/army-using-ground-penetrating-radar-to-look-for-agent-orange-at-korea-base-1.145330 (accessed 17 April 2012).

Schiller, Dane. "ICE Agent Wounded in Mexico Attack Released from Houston Hospital." *Houston Chronicle.* 15 February 2011. http://www.chron.com/ news/article/ICE-agent-wounded-in-mexico-released-from-1682313.php (accessed 4 September 2011).

Schultz, Teri. "More Drones Patrolling U.S.-Mexico Border." *Tuscon Sentinel.* 7
    December 2011. www.tusconsentinel.com/local/report/120711_border_
    drones/more-drones-patrolling-us-mexico-border/ (accessed 9 December 2011).

Seelke, Clare R. *U.S.-Mexican Security Cooperation: The Merida Initiative and Beyond.*
    Washington, DC: Congressional Research Service. 2011.

Serrano, Richard A. "Mexican Cartels Setting Up Shop Across U.S." *Los Angeles Times.*
    17 April 2011. http://articles.latimes.com/2011/apr/17/nation/la-na-crack-house-
    20110417 (accessed 17 April 2012).

Sourcebook of Criminal Justice Statistics Online. 2011. http://www.albany.edu/
    sourcebook/pdf/t1142012.pdf (accessed 14 November 2011).

St. Petersburg Times. "Politifact.com Truth-o-meter." 29 July 2010.
    http://www.politifact.com/truth-o-meter/statements/2010/john-mccain/john-
    mccain-said-he-would-add-3000-troops-border-w/ (accessed 23 October 2011).

TCOM. "TCOM, Aerostats." 2011. www.tcomlp.com/aerostats.html (accessed 7
    December 2011).

Titus, Elizabeth. "Lawmakers Want Defense Technology On Border." *Tuscon Sentinel.*
    18 November 2011. www.tusconsnetinel.com/nationworld/report/
    111811_border_defense_technology/lawmakers-want-defense-technology-border/
    (accessed 8 December 2011).

United States Border Patrol. *Border Patrol Agent Staffing by Fiscal Year.* Washington,
    DC: Department of Homeland Security. 2011.

————. *Enacted Border Patrol Program Budget by Fiscal Year.* Washington, DC:
    Department of Homeland Security. 2011.

————. *Illegal Alien Apprehensions From Mexico By Fiscal Year.* Washington, DC:
    Department of Homeland Security. 2011.

United States Census Bureau. *Foreign Trade: U.S. Trade with Mexico.* Washington, DC:
    Department of Commerce. 2012.

United States Customs and Border Protection. *Secure Borders. Safe Travel. Legal Trade:
    U.S. Customs and Border Protection Fiscal Year 2009-2014 Strategic Plan.*
    Washington, DC: Department of Homeland Security. 2008.

Xu, Jiaquan, Kenneth D.Kochanek, Sherry L. Murphy, and Betzaida Tejada-Vera.
    National Vital Statistics Reports 58, no. 19. Washington, DC: National Center for
    Health Statistics, 2010.

www.ingramcontent.com/pod-product-compliance
Lightning Source LLC
Chambersburg PA
CBHW081224170526
45165CB00009B/2946